OCEAN EXPLORER

SUE NICHOLSON

 Tangerine Press™

Congratulations! You've been selected to take part in a three-week exploration of the Earth's oceans, giving you the opportunity of seeing and studying some amazing marine creatures and finding out how they have adapted to life in different environments.

In particular, we would like you to try to spot a blue whale, and report back to the research center on the sighting and location.

Please check the enclosed tickets and itinerary carefully and study the suggested packing list. A pack of background information is included to get you started.

We look forward to welcoming you on board the research ship on March 1. Good luck!

Yours sincerely,

D. Adams

Douglas Adams (Research Officer)

A. Deveney

Abby Deveney (Research Officer)

The world's largest mammal

The blue whale, at 75–100 ft. (23–32 m) long and weighing up to 150 ton (144 tonnes), is the largest mammal ever to have lived on Earth. It is one of six species of rorqual whales, along with minke, humpback, and sei whales. Rorquals are filter feeders. They cruise through nutrient-rich polar waters, mouths open, filtering seawater through more than 300 baleen plates on each side of their jaws. Blue whales catch around four tons of tiny shrimps in these bristly fringes every day. When ice starts to cover their feeding grounds, blue whales migrate toward the Equator, where they mate. Calves are born in warm tropical waters the following year. Blue whales living in the northern hemisphere never meet the ones living in the southern hemisphere because they each migrate toward the tropics at different times of year. Even though blue whales have been a protected species since 1967, their numbers are still low, and the species may be in danger of extinction.

Itinerary

Day 1: Arrival and orientation
Rendezvous with the research ship off the islands of the Azores, Atlantic Ocean
• Facts and figures on the world's oceans and seas • Ocean floor

Day 2: Seashore
Exploration of seashore creatures on rocky coastline
• Tides • Crustaceans • Seabirds • Mollusks
• Shore zones • Mangroves • Plankton

Day 4: Out at sea
Observation of Atlantic marine life in the open ocean
• Ocean zones • Seaweed • Food chains and food webs • Upwelling • How fish swim • Parts of a fish • Camouflage • Types of fish • Ocean migration • Sea mammals • Overfishing

Day 6: Deep water
Descend in submersible to explore the deepsea marine life in Atlantic Ocean
• Deepsea life • Deepsea exploration

Day 10: The Great Barrier Reef
Exploration of the Great Barrier Reef off the northeastern coast of Queensland, Australia
• Coral reef zones • Types of reef • Hard and soft corals • How coral forms • Reef life • Shells • Sharks • Rays • Crown of Thorns starfish

Day 14: Black smokers
Rendezvous with second research ship on the East Pacific Rise and descend in submersible to explore marine life around hydrothermal vents
• Submersible facts and figures • Seafloor spreading • Black smokers • Tubeworms
• Vent life • Vent bacteria

Day 18: Antarctica
Exploration of Antarctic wildlife, on Ross Island in the Ross Sea, South Pacific Ocean
• Antarctica facts and figures • Seals • Whales
• Emperor Penguins • Distribution of krill
• Antarctic life

Day 21: Departure
• Whaling • Conserving the Antarctic

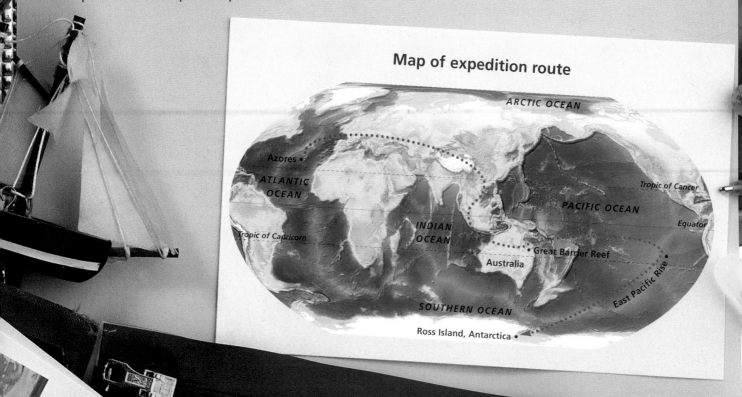

Map of expedition route

ARCTIC OCEAN

Azores •

ATLANTIC OCEAN

Tropic of Cancer

PACIFIC OCEAN

Equator

Tropic of Capricorn

INDIAN OCEAN

• Great Barrier Reef

Australia

East Pacific Rise

SOUTHERN OCEAN

Ross Island, Antarctica •

Suggested packing list

Equipment:
- Snorkel, mask, and fins*
- Underwater camera with flash
- Binoculars   ← *Take polaroid camera for instant photos!*
- Camera

- Sunglasses
- Sunscreen lotion   ← *Don't forget seasickness tablets!*
- First-aid kit

- Watercolor paints
- Pens and colored pencils
- Sketchpad
- Notebook
- Clipboard
- Reference book on marine animals

Get more film!

Clothing:
- Changes of warm clothing
- One change of lightweight clothing
- Underwear and socks
- Boots
- Deck shoes
- Swimsuit
- Warm weather gear for Antarctic:
  - Fiber-filled waterproof jacket (with fur hood)
  - Wind pants
  - Thermal long johns and vest
  - Thermal hat
  - Thermal socks
  - Gloves and glove liners
  - Snow goggles
  - Polar fleece jacket
  - Long-sleeved wool shirt and jeans

* Take walkman and tapes?

* Please note: Lifejackets and wetsuits will be provided by the research center.

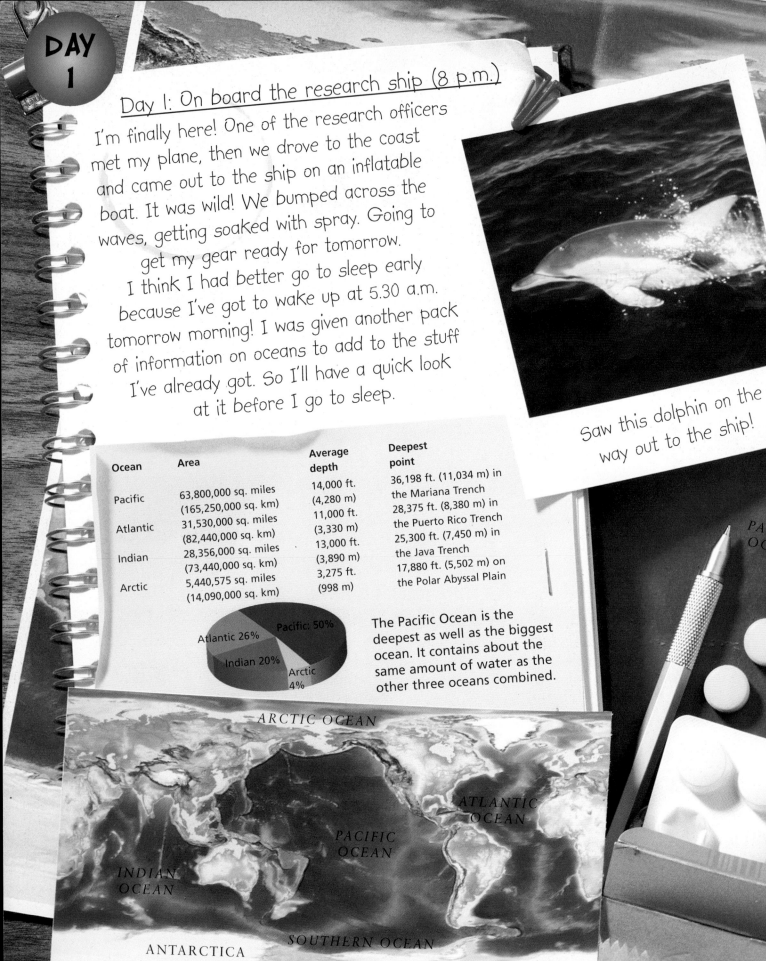

Day 1: On board the research ship (8 p.m.)

I'm finally here! One of the research officers met my plane, then we drove to the coast and came out to the ship on an inflatable boat. It was wild! We bumped across the waves, getting soaked with spray. Going to get my gear ready for tomorrow.
I think I had better go to sleep early because I've got to wake up at 5.30 a.m. tomorrow morning! I was given another pack of information on oceans to add to the stuff I've already got. So I'll have a quick look at it before I go to sleep.

Saw this dolphin on the way out to the ship!

Ocean	Area	Average depth	Deepest point
Pacific	63,800,000 sq. miles (165,250,000 sq. km)	14,000 ft. (4,280 m)	36,198 ft. (11,034 m) in the Mariana Trench
Atlantic	31,530,000 sq. miles (82,440,000 sq. km)	11,000 ft. (3,330 m)	28,375 ft. (8,380 m) in the Puerto Rico Trench
Indian	28,356,000 sq. miles (73,440,000 sq. km)	13,000 ft. (3,890 m)	25,300 ft. (7,450 m) in the Java Trench
Arctic	5,440,575 sq. miles (14,090,000 sq. km)	3,275 ft. (998 m)	17,880 ft. (5,502 m) on the Polar Abyssal Plain

Pacific: 50%
Atlantic 26%
Indian 20%
Arctic 4%

The Pacific Ocean is the deepest as well as the biggest ocean. It contains about the same amount of water as the other three oceans combined.

ARCTIC OCEAN

ATLANTIC OCEAN

PACIFIC OCEAN

INDIAN OCEAN

ANTARCTICA

SOUTHERN OCEAN

PACIFIC OCEAN

The Southern Ocean around Antarctica is not usually recognized as a true ocean in its own right. It is an extension of the Pacific, Atlantic, and Indian oceans.

I've taken two of these seasickness tablets already!

ARCTIC OCEAN

GREENLAND

NORTH
AMERICA

ATLANTIC
OCEAN

The → Azores
WE ARE
HERE!

AFRICA

SOUTH
AMERICA

Earth's oceans and seas as seen from space.

Our blue planet

An astronaut's view of the Earth looking down on the Pacific Ocean suggests that the planet's surface is almost entirely covered with water. In fact, the mighty Pacific covers just over one-third of the Earth's surface. Together, all the oceans take up over 70%, or more than two-thirds, of the world's surface.

Below the sea's surface

Have just *been* reading that the bottom of the ocean has flat plains, valleys, hills, mountains, and volcanoes – just like on dry land!

• In some places, the oceans are getting wider as magma (hot rock) bubbles up from *below* the Earth's crust, then cools and hardens into new oceanic crust.

• In other places, the ocean floor is sinking, forming deep ocean trenches.

Land

Continental shelf

Ocean ridge

Ocean trench

Continental slope

Seamounts (underwater volcanoes)

Volcanic islands

Abyssal plain

Apparently the world under the oceans is sometimes called "inner space." Oceanographers have mapped most of the ocean floor, but there's still a lot to discover...

9

Spotted this starfish stranded on a rock. It may dry out and die before the tide comes back in...

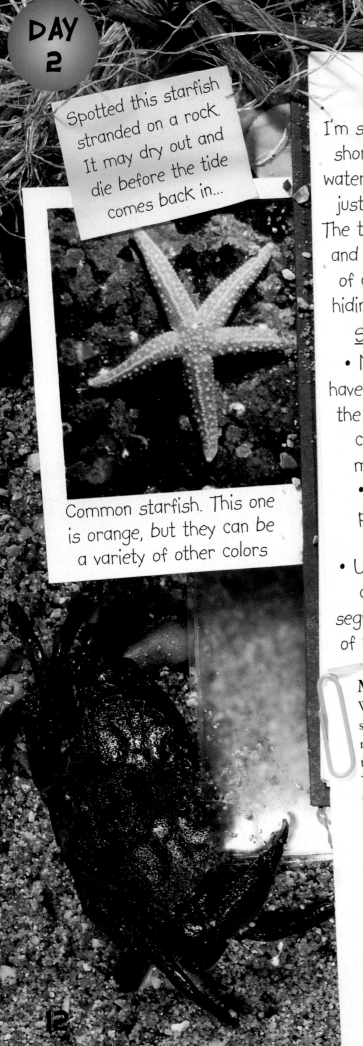

Common starfish. This one is orange, but they can be a variety of other colors

Day 2:
On the shore

I'm sitting in the middle shore zone where the water covered the rocks just a few hours ago. The tide's gone right out, and there are all kinds of amazing creatures hiding in the rockpools.

Shore crab study

• Nine legs – should have five pairs (including the pincers), but many crabs have one or more legs missing.
• Hard shell gives protection against predators.
• Underneath the body are folded several segments – the remains of the crab's abdomen.

(Picked up my crab by its shell from behind so I didn't get pinched!)

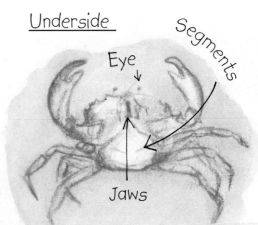

Two pairs of antennae

Pincer (to pick up food)

Jointed leg

Claw

Top side

Hard shell (called a carapace) – 3 in. (8 cm) wide

Underside

Eye

Segments

Jaws

Mangrove swamps

While rocky shores are constantly eroded by the sea, in other places shores are built up by pebbles or sand or by muddy deposits from rivers. Plants growing on mud flats help to hold the mud and prevent the erosion of the coastline. Mangrove trees grow in the tropics. Their long roots are partly covered by tidal waters but stick up above the mud so they can take in oxygen from the air. Mangroves provide homes for many marine creatures, including young shellfish.

Gull's feather

There are loads of herring gulls wheeling overhead. They're REALLY noisy. These birds are aerial feeders – they fly in search of food, plucking fish out of the water or snatching other birds' eggs or chicks.

Black-headed gull with long, narrow wings

Acorn barnacle

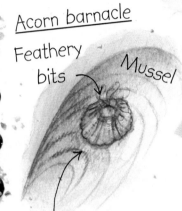

Feathery bits

Mussel

Attaches itself fast to mussel shell

I've been looking through a magnifying glass at tiny white acorn barnacles clinging to the shells of mussels. The barnacle shell opens, and the animal starts feeding on microscopic plankton when the tide comes in.

High tide, low tide

Twice a day, the ocean rises on the shore until it reaches the high tide mark. Then it falls back until it reaches the low tide mark. Seashore creatures from sand worms to shellfish are battered by crashing waves and shifting sand as the tide ebbs and flows, and are alternately submerged in salty seawater, then exposed to icy cold air or the hot, drying sun, depending on the time of year. As a result, seashore animals have developed different ways of surviving the pounding waves, exposure to the air, and rapid changes in temperature.

Barnacles glue themselves to rocks or shells so they are not dislodged by the tide.

Ruddy turnstone

The turnstone winters on rocky shores. It turns over stones and debris along the coast to uncover crustaceans and mollusks to feed on. In summer, it breeds on marshes or in the tundra of the Arctic coast.

Eurasian oystercatcher

The oystercatcher breeds in Eurasia. It may winter as far south as Africa, India, or southern China. It feeds mainly on mollusks and crustaceans, poking in the mud or prying shellfish off the rocks with its long, flattened bill.

Rocky shore zones

There are four zones on rocky shores:
- the splash zone, above the high-tide level, which is covered only by the highest tides in a month.
- the upper shore, between the highest and lowest high tides, which is uncovered most of the time.
- the middle shore, between the high and low tides, which is uncovered by the sea for around half of the time in a given month.
- the lower shore, near the low-tide level, which is uncovered only by the lowest tides in a month.

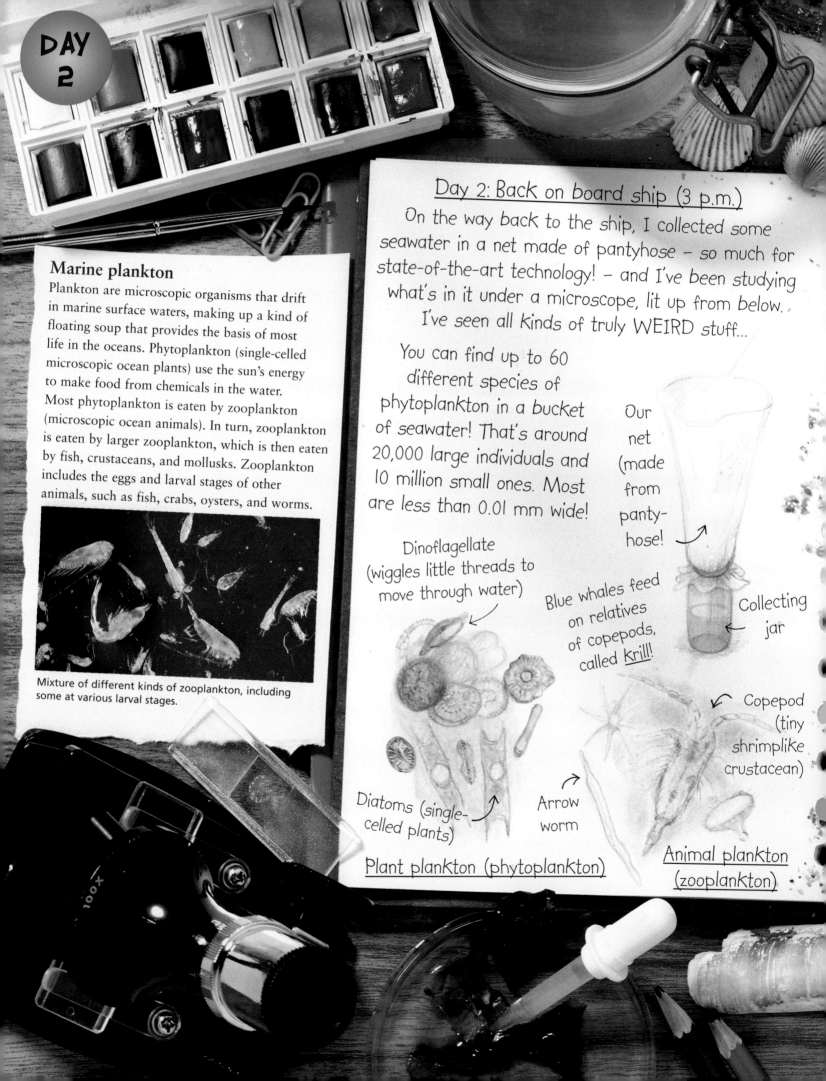

Marine plankton

Plankton are microscopic organisms that drift in marine surface waters, making up a kind of floating soup that provides the basis of most life in the oceans. Phytoplankton (single-celled microscopic ocean plants) use the sun's energy to make food from chemicals in the water. Most phytoplankton is eaten by zooplankton (microscopic ocean animals). In turn, zooplankton is eaten by larger zooplankton, which is then eaten by fish, crustaceans, and mollusks. Zooplankton includes the eggs and larval stages of other animals, such as fish, crabs, oysters, and worms.

Mixture of different kinds of zooplankton, including some at various larval stages.

Day 2: Back on board ship (3 p.m.)

On the way back to the ship, I collected some seawater in a net made of pantyhose – so much for state-of-the-art technology! – and I've been studying what's in it under a microscope, lit up from below. I've seen all kinds of truly WEIRD stuff...

You can find up to 60 different species of phytoplankton in a bucket of seawater! That's around 20,000 large individuals and 10 million small ones. Most are less than 0.01 mm wide!

Our net (made from panty-hose!

Collecting jar

Dinoflagellate (wiggles little threads to move through water)

Blue whales feed on relatives of copepods, called <u>krill</u>!

Copepod (tiny shrimplike crustacean)

Diatoms (single-celled plants)

Arrow worm

Plant plankton (phytoplankton)

Animal plankton (zooplankton)

Cuttlefish bone
washed up on shore

Cuttlefish

Despite its name, the cuttlefish is a mollusk, not a fish. Like its relative, the squid, it has eight arms and two long tentacles, which it uses to catch crabs and other prey.

Fleshy fins for swimming through water

Big eyes

Mouth surrounded by tentacles with suckers

Empty cockle shell

Shells

Some of the empty shells I've found washed up on the beach would once have had two parts, hinged at the top or side. These <u>bivalve mollusks</u> dig down into the sand. Cockles filter food through their gills. Water and food enters through a tube called a <u>siphon</u>.

Live cockle

Leathery, elastic hinge joins two halves of shell at top

Muscular foot to dig down into sand

Muscles hold the shell tightly closed if disturbed

Cockle shells

Giant clam bath

Villagers in the Indo-Pacific islands have a luxurious way of taking a bath – in the shell of a giant clam! Islanders eat the clam's tender flesh, then use the empty shells as bathtubs. Giant clams can grow up to 5 ft. (1.5 m) long, making them the world's largest bivalves. Like other clams, the giant clam feeds on plankton that it filters out of the water. It also feeds on nutrients made by tiny algae living in the mantle (tissue lining the inside of its shell).

Razor shells

2 siphons

Mussels

Anchor themselves to rocks by lots of thin, tough threads made of a liquid that hardens in water.

Muscular foot

Feed at high tide when covered by water

Filter nutrients from seawater

Mussels

Razor shell - lives vertically in the sand

Bottlenose dolphins

Short-finned pilot whale

One of a group of ten or so – they're very sociable and often swim with bottlenose dolphins

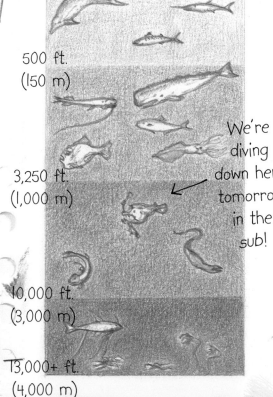

Manx shearwater taking off

↑ Watched this shearwater dive right into the water and pluck out a fish!

Day 4: Out at sea

We've been sailing out into open waters all morning. I've been sitting up on the deck, keeping a lookout for birds and fish. I've made two BRILLIANT sightings – a school of bottlenose dolphins, which came really close to the boat, and a pilot whale! Little chance of spotting a blue whale, though, because most will be farther south, only coming north in a month or so to get to their Arctic feeding grounds.

Ocean zones

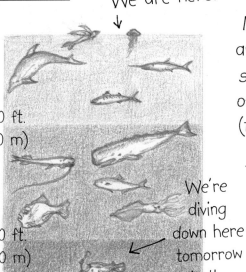

We are here!
↓

500 ft. (150 m)

3,250 ft. (1,000 m)

We're diving down here tomorrow in the sub!

10,000 ft. (3,000 m)

13,000+ ft. (4,000 m)

Epipelagic zone
Most plants and animals live in this sunlit, upper part of the open ocean (to 500 ft./150 m)

Mesopelagic zone
Twilight zone (500–3,250 ft./ 150–1,000 m)

Bathypelagic zone
Pitch black (3,250–10,000 ft./ 1,000–3,000 m)

Abyssopelagic zone
(13,000 ft./3,000 m down to bottom)

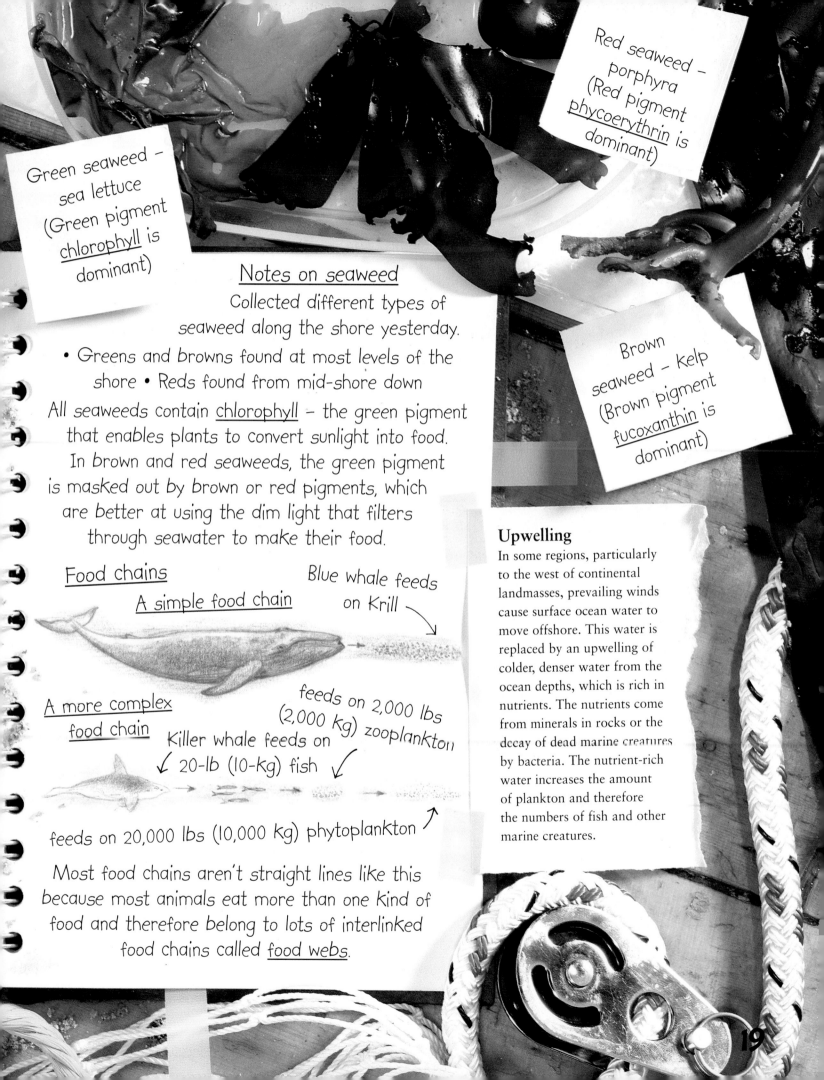

Green seaweed – sea lettuce (Green pigment <u>chlorophyll</u> is dominant)

Red seaweed – porphyra (Red pigment <u>phycoerythrin</u> is dominant)

Notes on seaweed

Collected different types of seaweed along the shore yesterday.

• Greens and browns found at most levels of the shore • Reds found from mid-shore down

All seaweeds contain <u>chlorophyll</u> – the green pigment that enables plants to convert sunlight into food. In brown and red seaweeds, the green pigment is masked out by brown or red pigments, which are better at using the dim light that filters through seawater to make their food.

Brown seaweed – kelp (Brown pigment <u>fucoxanthin</u> is dominant)

<u>Food chains</u>

<u>A simple food chain</u>

Blue whale feeds on Krill

feeds on 2,000 lbs (2,000 kg) zooplankton

<u>A more complex food chain</u>

Killer whale feeds on 20-lb (10-kg) fish

feeds on 20,000 lbs (10,000 kg) phytoplankton

Most food chains aren't straight lines like this because most animals eat more than one kind of food and therefore belong to lots of interlinked food chains called <u>food webs</u>.

Upwelling

In some regions, particularly to the west of continental landmasses, prevailing winds cause surface ocean water to move offshore. This water is replaced by an upwelling of colder, denser water from the ocean depths, which is rich in nutrients. The nutrients come from minerals in rocks or the decay of dead marine creatures by bacteria. The nutrient-rich water increases the amount of plankton and therefore the numbers of fish and other marine creatures.

Notes on fish

There are around 25,000 different kinds of fish living in the world's oceans, seas, lakes, rivers, and streams.

Breathing: As a fish swims, it takes in water through its mouth and pushes it out through gill slits on each side of its head. Oxygen passes from the water into the fish's blood inside the gills.

Scales: Overlapping scales help protect the fish and help it move faster through water. Slimy mucus covering the scales keeps them moist and clean.

Bony fish shape
(a sock-eye salmon)

Dark back

Light-colored belly

Lateral line

Countershading: Many fish have dark backs to blend in with dark depths below, and light-colored bellies to blend in with brighter, sunlit water above.

Lateral line: Row of nerve endings running from head to tail along fish's sides helping it sense movement and vibrations in the water.

How a fish swims

Fast-swimming fish power through the water by beating their tail fins from side to side. Slower swimmers bend their bodies from side to side, too. Other fins are used to keep balance, change direction, and slow down. Pectoral fins change a fish's pitch (vertical angle).

Pitch

← Pectoral fin

Dolphins (mammals, not fish) move their tails up and down, not side to side, to push themselves forward

Camouflage

Some bottom-living fish, such as halibut, plaice, and flounder, can change their colors and markings to blend in with the surrounding seabed and hide from predators.

Peacock flounder

PARTS OF A FISH

Gill cover
(over gill
slits)

Eye

Dorsal fin

Caudal fin, or tail fin

Lateral line

Mouth

Pectoral fin

Scales

Anal fin

Pelvic fin

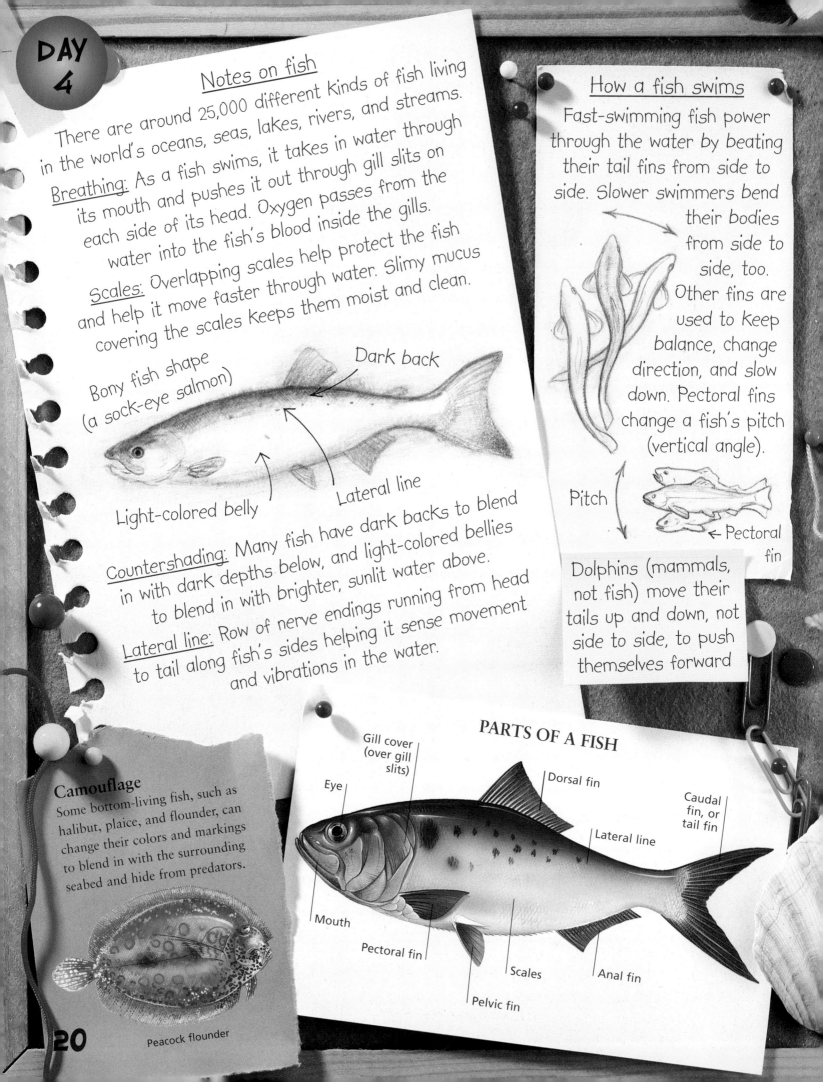

Migration

Many marine creatures migrate. Some sea journeys are quite short – squid, fish, and shrimp swim up from the sea's middle depths each night to feed on zooplankton near the sea's surface. Other journeys are incredibly long, with animals traveling immense distances.

Green turtles

Sea turtles spend all their lives in the water, only leaving it to lay eggs on shore. Some female green turtles migrate more than 1,250 miles (2,000 km) to lay their eggs on the beach where they hatched. Scientists do not know how they find their way through the ocean. They may use a strong sense of smell, or navigate using a biological magnetic compass inside the body.

Gray whales

Every year, gray whales in the eastern North Pacific Ocean swim about 14,000 miles (22,000 km) between their breeding grounds off the coast of California and their feeding grounds in the Arctic, near Alaska, and back again. They spend the summer months feeding in the food-rich waters of the Arctic before returning to the breeding grounds to mate.

Arctic terns

The Arctic tern flies over 22,000 miles (35,000 km) a year, from the Arctic to the Antarctic and back again, to take advantage of the plentiful food available during the short summer in each region.

Fish bone with tail attached

European eels

European eels lay their eggs in the Sargasso Sea in the Atlantic Ocean. The eggs hatch into larvae, which slowly drift on ocean currents to coastal estuaries and river mouths. There, the larvae metamorphose (change) into elvers, or young eels. The elvers swim upstream, where they grow and mature. When they become adults, the eels migrate down the rivers and back to the Sargasso Sea, where they lay their eggs and die.

Elvers resting on journey upstream.

March of the spiny lobsters

Every fall, spiny lobsters living off the coast of Florida migrate along the seabed in groups of around 100,000 or so. The journey takes about a month. To protect themselves from predators, the lobsters march in single file in lines of up to 60, with each lobster's antennae touching the tail of the lobster in front.

Spiny lobsters marching on seabed.

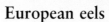

Types of fish

There are three main groups of fish:

Cartilaginous fish (around 850 species) have skeletons made of cartilage rather than bone and include sharks, skates, and rays. Unlike bony fish, they don't have gas-filled swim bladders, so they need to keep swimming; otherwise, they will sink. All cartilaginous fish live in the sea, and most are active predators.

Blue shark

Bony fish (around 25,000 species) have bony skeletons and fin rays. They can adjust the amount of gas in their swim bladders so that they can rest or stay motionless in the water. Some bony fish feed on plants. Others are fast-swimming predators with sharp teeth. Some predators use camouflage to hide in wait for passing prey.

Zander

Primitive fish (around 60 species) include lampreys and hagfishes. Lampreys have jawless, suckerlike mouths that they clamp onto other fishes, to feed on their blood. Hagfishes don't have jaws either. They bore into the bodies of dead or dying fishes and eat them from the inside out.

River lamprey

Whale shark

Range: All tropical seas
Habitat: Surface waters
Food: Small fish and plankton
Size: 50 ft. (15 m)
Features: The world's largest living fish.

Empty crab shell that I found

Mako shark

Range: Atlantic, Pacific, and India oceans: temperate and tropical areas
Habitat: Open sea
Food: Surface-living fish (such as tuna, mackerel, herring, and squid)
Size: 6–12 ft. (2–4 m)
Features: Pointed snout and powerful, streamlined body.

Atlantic halibut

Range: North Atlantic Ocean
Habitat: Sandy-, gravel- and rocky-bottomed waters at 300–5,000 ft. (100–1,500 m)
Food: Fish; young halibuts also feed on crustaceans
Size: 6–8 ft. (2–2.4 m)
Features: The largest of the flatfish. It cannot reproduce until it is between 10 and 14 years old.

Atlantic mackerel

Range: Atlantic Ocean, Mediterranean Sea
Habitat: Offshore surface waters
Food: Crustaceans and small fish
Size: 16–26 in. (41–66 cm)
Features: Goes north to breed in spring and summer, and returns south in winter.

Cuttlefish bone

Flying fish

Range: All tropical and subtropical oceans
Habitat: Open sea
Food: Other fish
Size: 12 in. (30 cm)
Features: Has one pair of "wings" (enlarged pectoral fins), so its flights are shorter and less controlled than those made by four-winged flying fish.

Ocean sunfish

Range: Atlantic, Pacific, and Indian oceans: temperate and tropical areas
Habitat: Open sea
Food: Small plankton, such as jellyfish, crustaceans, and fish
Size: Up to 13 ft. (4 m)
Features: Has an almost circular body, which ends in a frill rather than a tail.

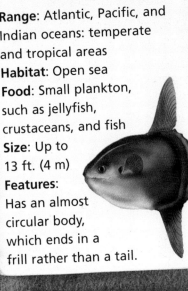

Toothed and baleen whales

Like all mammals, whales and dolphins are air-breathing, warm-bloodied animals, and they give birth to live young.

There are two groups of whales: toothed whales (about 80 species) and baleen whales (about 12 species). Cuvier's beaked whale is a toothed whale. It grows to around 20–23 ft. (6–7 m) and has an elongated snout. It feeds on deep-water fish and squid. The minke whale is a baleen whale and grows to around 26–33 ft. (8–10 m). It has a pointed snout, with about 300 baleen plates on each side of its jaws and 60 to 70 grooves on its throat.

Cuvier's beaked whale

Minke whale

Skate

Range: East Atlantic Ocean, Mediterranean Sea
Habitat: Seafloor at moderate depths
Food: Fish, crabs, lobsters, and octopus
Size: 8 ft. (2.4 m)
Features: Has a flat body and a tail covered with spines to help defend it against attackers; bottom-dwelling fish.

Purple jellyfish

Range: Atlantic, Pacific, and Indian oceans
Habitat: Open sea, surface, and middle waters
Food: Plankton
Size: Bell up to 4 in. (10 cm) wide; tentacles 36 in. (90 cm) long
Features: Stinging cells give protection and paralyze prey.

Swordfish

Range: Worldwide, temperate and tropical seas
Habitat: Open sea, surface, and middle waters
Food: Fish and squid
Size: 6–15 ft. (2–4.9 m)
Features: Has an elongated, flattened snout to strike prey and a streamlined shape to help it move easily through the water.

Overfishing warnings

Environmental report

Intensive fishing has threatened many of our ocean resources. Every year, around 75 million tons of fish are caught worldwide for food. There are two main types of food fish: pelagic fish that live near the surface, including tuna, mackerel, and herring, and bottom-living demersal fish, including cod, flounder, plaice, and halibut, and shellfish, such as lobsters and crabs.

Overfishing of some species is a serious problem. "They are being taken from the sea too fast for them to reproduce," warned one oceanographer. "The Atlantic halibut, for example, is particularly threatened because of its slow rate of growth and late maturity."

Crew hauling in their catch.

Cockle shells

Day 6: Deep water

I'm in the submersible, 7,000 ft. (2,200 m) below the sea's surface! It's a bit cramped – and chilly because we're in such deep, cold water. I've been peering out of the porthole, trying to spot some fish. Some look really weird with tiny spines on their backs or heads, a bit like fishing rods. Most deepsea fish are small (not much bigger than my hand) – larger fish wouldn't find enough food to survive. They feed on other fish and dead animals and plants floating down from surface waters.

Fishing rod lure

Creatures come to the lure, thinking its food, then get snapped up in the angler's jaws!

Angler fish

Deepsea shrimp

Range: Atlantic Ocean
Habitat: Deep sea
Food: Any dead and decaying matter raining down from surface waters
Size: Up to 4 in. (10 cm) long
Features: Has antennae longer than its body to help it find food in dark waters.

Sloane's viperfish

Range: All oceans: tropical and subtropical areas
Habitat: Deep sea
Food: Smaller fish
Size: 12 in. (30 cm)
Features: Has long, fanglike teeth and a skull adapted to increase the width its jaw can open. Has a light-producing organ attached to its dorsal fin.

Notes on lanternfish

• Between 4 and 8 in. (10 and 20 cm) long • Feeds on zooplankton • Large eyes for its size • Lives in schools

Photophones

• Light-producing organs (called photophones) arranged in short rows and groups on its body
• In pitch-black water, lights can be used to:
1. find a mate 2. find prey 3. confuse its enemies (lanternfish sometimes lash their tails from side to side to dazzle predators)

Bottom-dwellers

Some fish and other creatures can survive the immense water pressure at incredible depths of 10,000 to 20,000 ft. (3,000 to 6,000 m) on the abyssal plain, in near-freezing, pitch-black water.

Brittlestar

The brittlestar lives in the dark depths of the Atlantic Ocean. Its disklike body is 1 in. (2.5 cm) wide, and it has five long, spiny arms each up to 4 in. (10 cm) long. The brittle star's mouth is under its body.

The sea cucumber, which is related to the starfish, lives on the seabed of the Atlantic Ocean. It can grow up to 10 in. (25 cm) long. Its body has rows of tiny tube feet all along it, and its mouth is surrounded by food-gathering tentacles.

Sea cucumber

The tripod fish lives in all oceans in deep waters and on the seabed and grows up to 12 in. (30 cm) long. It rests on stiffened fins on the seafloor, waiting for a passing meal, such as a small crustacean.

Tripod fish

Deepsea exploration

In 1960, the bathyscaphe *Trieste*, with a crew of two, dived nearly 36,000 ft. (11,000 m) to the seabed in the Mariana Trench, the deepest part of the Pacific Ocean. It took nearly five hours to reach the bottom. In 1995, the research submersible *Kaiko* repeated the journey, but this time uncrewed. It discovered shrimp, sea cucumbers, and jellyfish on the seabed.

Kaiko, a remote-controlled vehicle.

A gulper eel! Has big jaws to swallow prey whole and an elastic stomach that stretches to digest it! Yuk! ↓

Giant squid

Range: Atlantic Ocean
Habitat: Open sea
Food: Fish and crustaceans
Size: Up to 60 ft. (18 m)
Features: Has two tentacles and eight sucker-covered arms; moves by shooting water out of its body through a funnel.

27

Day 10: The Great Barrier Reef

It's been a fantastic day, snorkeling on the reef! It's really quiet once you're underwater and SO COLORFUL. Little fish swam right up to my mask, and a cleaner prawn tried to groom my hand!

Saw a sea anemone feed...

Anemone gobbling up a fish! YUK!

Some shrimp and fish groom predators that otherwise would eat them! Abby (the research officer) pointed out a stonefish hiding in the rocks below – lethal if you tread on one because their spines inject you with poison.

Cone shell DANGEROUS! Can shoot out poison!

Miter shell

Abby has given me these (empty) shells to look at. We didn't pick up any on the reef in case we harmed the animals living in them. Also, some are REALLY dangerous!

Coral reef zones

Back reef

Reef flat

Abyssal ridge

Buttress zone

Fore reef zone

Calmer waters

More waves (lots of coral, sponges, sea urchins, and fish here)

Strong waves and currents here

We dived mostly in the reef flat

Fore reef has lots of staghorn, sea fan, and gorgonian corals

65 ft. (20 m)

165 ft. (50 m)

230 ft. (70 m)

500 ft. (150 m)

A coral polyp

A reef is made up of lots of tiny polyps like this one

Tentacles sting passing prey and draw it into gut

Gut digests polyp's food (but nutrients from food pass to the whole coral colony)

"Mouth" of polyp opens (mainly at night)

Algae live inside each polyp. They provide plant food and oxygen for the coral, and the coral provides nutrients and carbon dioxide for the algae.

As they grow, the polyps form little limestone cups. These stony skeletons are left behind when the polyps die, and new colonies grow on them.

Spider shell – closes shell with strong foot

Tiger cowrie – mostly comes out at night to feed

Reef life spotter's guide

Reefs are teeming with life, and competition for space is fierce. Many fish are armed with weapons or are brightly colored and patterned to warn potential predators that they are dangerous, to camouflage themselves from their enemies, or to identify and attract a mate of the same species. Some reef creatures have developed unusual symbiotic partnerships. For example, clownfish live among the poisonous tentacles of the sea anemone without being stung. In return, the fish helps to keep the anemone clean, and the anemone also feeds on scraps of food left over by the fish.

Clown anemone fish
Its body is covered in slime to protect it from the anemone's stinging tentacles.

Copperband butterfly fish
A black spot near its dorsal fin confuses predators into thinking this is the vulnerable head. It has a beaked snout so it can reach into crevices to find food.

Lionfish
Brightly colored stripes warn enemies that its spines contain poisonous venom.

Clown triggerfish
Dramatic patterns on its body break up its outline and make it hard for a predator to find it against the coral. Its locking "trigger" spine allows it to wedge itself into crevices if threatened.

Coral reef distribution map

Reef-building hard corals can grow only in warm, sunlit water, where the temperature is at least 65°F (18°C) all year. They are therefore found mainly in the tropics on the east side of continents, where there are warmer ocean currents.

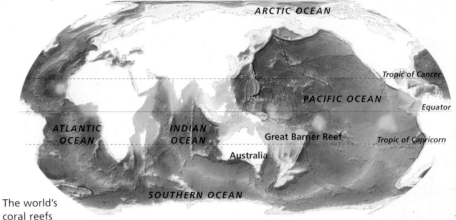

ARCTIC OCEAN

Tropic of Cancer

PACIFIC OCEAN

Equator

ATLANTIC OCEAN

INDIAN OCEAN

Great Barrier Reef

Tropic of Capricorn

Australia

SOUTHERN OCEAN

The world's coral reefs

Sea urchin

Range: All oceans
Habitat: Both hard and soft seabeds
Size: Body 4 in. (10 cm); spines 1 ½–16 in. (4–40 cm) long
Features: Member of the echinoderm group.

Types of reef

There are three main types of coral reef. As a volcanic island sinks, it forms each of the main types of reef.

Fringing reef

Grows in shallow water along the coast or around many tropical islands.

Barrier reef

Grows farther from the coast and rises more steeply from the sea in deeper water than a fringing reef; separated from the land by a lagoon of shallower, calmer water.

Atoll

Like a barrier reef, but circular or oval in shape; surrounds a lagoon that was once a central volcanic island that has sunk beneath the waves.

Hawksbill turtle

Range: Tropical Atlantic, Pacific, and Indian oceans; Caribbean sea
Habitat: Coral reefs, rocky coasts
Size: 30–36 in. (76–91 cm)
Features: Endangered because killed for its shell.

Sundial shell

Auger screw shell

Sharks

A variety of sharks live around coral reefs, but divers are unlikely to meet the larger ones. Great Barrier Reef sharks include hammerheads, white-tipped and black-tipped reef sharks, and the tessellated wobbegong, which camouflages itself on the seabed to escape from danger.

Hammerhead shark

Unlike hard corals, soft corals can grow in colder, deeper water where there is less sunlight.

Soft coral is made up of lots of polyps, but it doesn't form a hard limestone skeleton. It is protected by toxins or sharp needles.

<u>Staghorn coral</u> (or finger coral)
* Forms colonies around 3 ft. (1 m) wide • Grows in waters up to 150 ft. (48 m) deep

Branches (look like deer antlers or fingers)

<u>Brain coral</u>
* Lives in colonies around 3 ft. (1 m) wide
* Grows in water from 20–40 ft. (6–12 m) deep
* Lives in colonies around 6 ft. (1.8 m) wide

<u>Sheet coral</u>
* Grows in water between 65–120 ft. (20–36 m) deep

New reef colonies begin when the eggs of one polyp are fertilized by the sperm of another. Existing colonies grow by budding – when new polyps bud, or grow, from their parents – eventually forming colonies up to 10 ft. (3 m) wide.

Soft coral in the Great Barrier Reef – the largest reef system in the world at 1,250 miles (2,000 km) long!

Crown of Thorns starfish

Some marine scientists remain worried about the danger to coral reefs from the Crown of Thorns starfish. Just one of these 16-armed creatures can gobble up 10 sq. ft. (1 sq. m) of coral in a month. Sudden population increases of the starfish result in large patches of the reef being destroyed. However, most types of hard coral can recolonize these areas within 10 to 20 years.

The Crown of Thorns starfish eats by pulling its stomach out through its mouth, wrapping it over its prey, and digesting its meal before it pulls its stomach back inside.

Rays

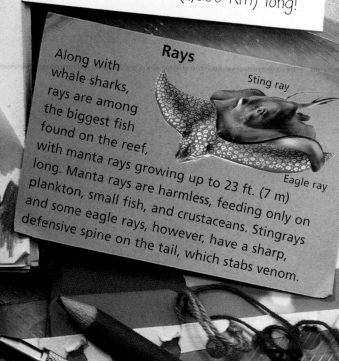

Sting ray

Eagle ray

Along with whale sharks, rays are among the biggest fish found on the reef, with manta rays growing up to 23 ft. (7 m) long. Manta rays are harmless, feeding only on plankton, small fish, and crustaceans. Stingrays and some eagle rays, however, have a sharp, defensive spine on the tail, which stabs venom.

Day 14

We met up with the second research ship out in the mid-Pacific yesterday, and now I'm back in a sub! It took us around two hours to reach the bottom. It got dark quite quickly and really cold. I've spent most of the time taking temperature and pressure readings, and peering out of the portholes, looking at some of the strange creatures living around the vents.

Best of all, I was allowed to operate the sub's robot arm to pick up rock samples from the seabed!

Here's our sub

Just three of us fit in here – I'm the only one who can actually stand up straight!

↙ Lights (the sub has lots!)

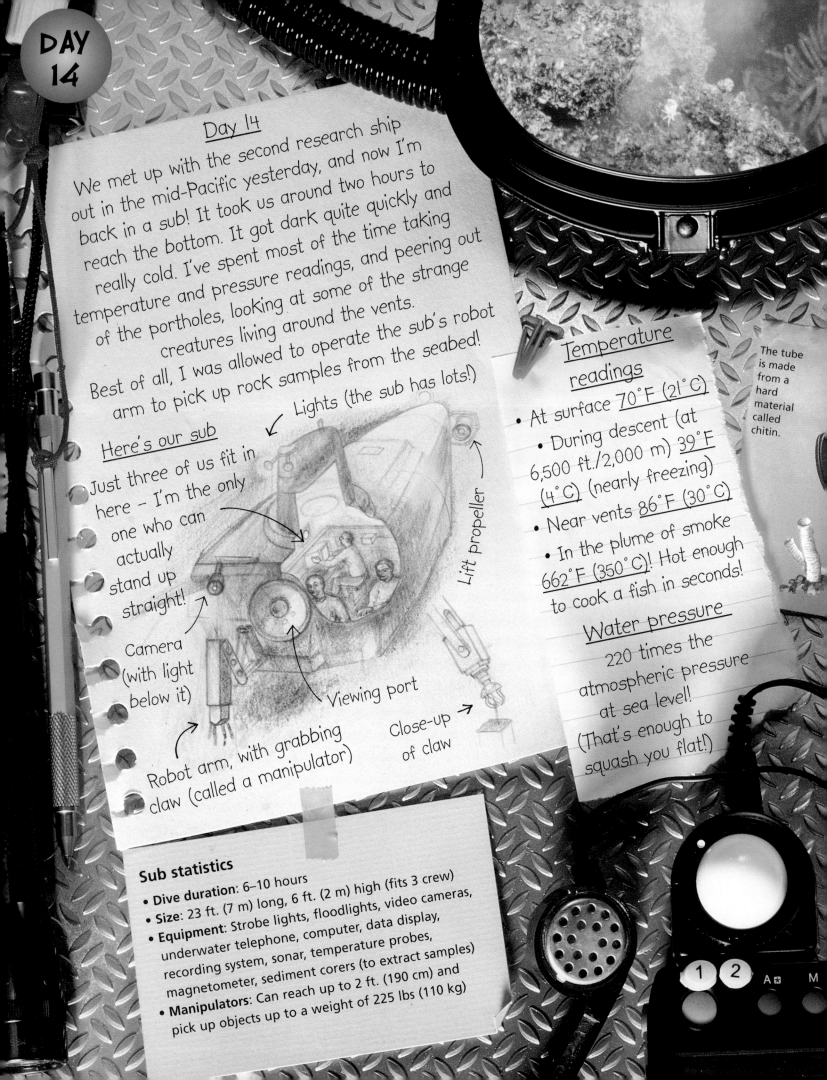

Lift propeller

Camera (with light below it)

Viewing port

Robot arm, with grabbing claw (called a manipulator)

Close-up → of claw

Temperature readings

- At surface 70°F (21°C)
- During descent (at 6,500 ft./2,000 m) 39°F (4°C) (nearly freezing)
- Near vents 86°F (30°C)
- In the plume of smoke 662°F (350°C)! Hot enough to cook a fish in seconds!

Water pressure

220 times the atmospheric pressure at sea level! (That's enough to squash you flat!)

The tube is made from a hard material called chitin.

Sub statistics

- **Dive duration:** 6–10 hours
- **Size:** 23 ft. (7 m) long, 6 ft. (2 m) high (fits 3 crew)
- **Equipment:** Strobe lights, floodlights, video cameras, underwater telephone, computer, data display, recording system, sonar, temperature probes, magnetometer, sediment corers (to extract samples)
- **Manipulators:** Can reach up to 2 ft. (190 cm) and pick up objects up to a weight of 225 lbs (110 kg)

Seafloor spreading

The Earth's crust is made up of a jigsaw of plates that slide on the molten rock of the mantle below. At places on the ocean floor, where two plates are slowly sliding away from each other, magma from below the crust rises along the split, spreads outward, then cools and hardens, forming new oceanic crust.

Ocean ridge
New crust
Oceanic crust
Mantle
Continental crust
Rising magma

Got a great view of a black smoker from one of the portholes!

Water is around 662°F (350°C)!

Black smokers

Creatures such as mussels (filter feeders) eat the bacteria that grow around the vents.

"Black smokers"

When hot water full of minerals spurts up through vents (cracks) in the ocean crust, and then cools down, it forms tall stacks, which can grow up to 30 ft. (10 m) tall. They are called "black smokers" because sulfur from the vents turns the water black.

Tubeworms

Tubeworm

Tube

Tubeworms make their tube homes around deepsea vents, using minerals taken from the water. The tubes, each up to 6 ft. (2 m) long, help protect the worms from predators, such as crab and fish. The worms don't eat – they have no mouths, guts, or bottoms. Instead, they take nutrients from bacteria living inside them. The worms depend completely on the bacteria for their nourishment. If the hot sulfur springs die, the bacteria die, too, and so do the worms.

Vent bacteria

Bacteria are at the base of the food chain near the deepsea vents. They multiply quickly in the water, which is full of sulfur, growing in clumps on rocks and inside some of the vent animals. Scientists estimate that there are millions of individual bacteria in every cubic inch of water, with hundreds of strains (or types) of different bacteria around the vents.

Vent life

Clams

Crab

Zoarcid fish

Vent creatures cluster in groups around vents. Clams live farther from the chimneys, in cracks between lumps of lava. They grow up to 1 ft. (30 cm) long and about 500 times faster than their relatives in other parts of the deep ocean. Crabs crawl all around the vents, feeding on tubeworms, shrimp, and mussels. Another predator, the Zoarcid fish (about 2 ft./60 cm long), lives around tubeworms.

37

Day 18: Antarctica

IT'S FREEZING! I'm wearing layers and layers of clothes and sun goggles because the sunlight really glares off the ice (AND it's light for 20 hours a day!) Flew in on a small airplane yesterday – it landed on skis on the ice! We've been out on a little boat called a Zodiac for some of the day, and I got really excited when we saw some whales – we were really close! They were humpbacks, though, not blue whales. One actually flipped out of the water and landed with a massive thud on its back. <u>Here it is!</u>

Also saw this young crabeater seal (the most common Antarctic seal) on the ice. It feeds mainly on krill. A layer of blubber under its skin and fur on its body and flippers keep it warm.

Humpbacked whale breaching

Antarctic facts

Area: 5,200,000 sq. miles (13.5 million sq. km)
Icecap: Approximately 7,200 ft. (2,200 m) thick, containing 90% of all ice on Earth
Winter temperature (July): -40°F to -95°F (-40°C to -70°C) inland and 5°F to -22°F (-15°C to -30°C) along coast
Summer temperature (January): 5°F to -30°F (-15°C to -35°C) inland and up to 50°F (10°C) along coast
Average wind speeds: 45 mph/70 km/h (making the icy Antarctic air feel even colder)
Highest elevation: Vinson Massif, 16,865 ft. (5,140 m) above sea level

Pack ice in March (end of Antarctic summer)

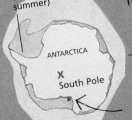

ANTARCTICA

X South Pole

Pack ice in October (height of Antarctic winter)

We are here!

Penguin city

Saw some Emperor penguins today – they're really big (about 3 ft./1 m tall). It's breeding time. The females will lay single eggs in May to early June, then go back to the sea until the chicks hatch in July. Meanwhile, the males huddle together on the ice throughout the freezing cold Antarctic winter, incubating the eggs on their feet!

Crabeater seal
Habitat: Edge of pack ice
Food: Mostly krill, which it strains from the water through its teeth
Size: 6–8 ft. (2–2.4 m)
Features: Few enemies, except orcas.

Leopard seal
Habitat: Pack ice, coasts, islands
Food: Penguins, fish, crustaceans, sometimes other seals
Size: 10–12 ft. (3–3.5 m)
Features: Large mouth for grasping prey.

Weddell seal
Habitat: Edge of pack ice
Food: Deep water fish, such as Antarctic cod
Size: Up to 10 ft. (2.9 m)
Features: Dives deeper than any other seal.

Antarctic life

Animals that live at the poles have adapted to icy conditions. Many Antarctic fish, such as icefish, have a kind of natural antifreeze in their blood. The blood of the Antarctic cod contains a special protein to lower its freezing point so the fish can survive in temperatures as low as 29°F (1.9°C).

Icefish

Mammals, such as seals and whales, rely on a thick insulating layer of fatty blubber under their skin. Seals also have fur on their bodies and flippers for extra warmth. Most animals can live in the Antarctic only because of the huge amount of plant plankton that grows in the icy sea in spring. Millions of tiny shrimplike creatures called krill feed on this plankton. Krill are the most important zooplankton in the Antarctic. Even though they are so small, krill are the main food of 5 species of whale, 20 species of fish, 3 species of seal, 3 species of squid, and lots of sea birds.

Antarctic cod

Antarctic krill

Krill distribution map

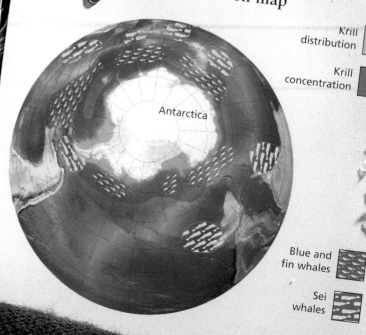

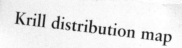

Krill distribution

Krill concentration

Antarctica

Blue and fin whales

Sei whales

Day 21: Going home!

Finally on my way home... We've been flying north in a small, light aircraft for around two hours and GUESS WHAT, I've just seen not one, but TWO blue whales!!! I spotted what looked like a plume of smoke far below in the ocean and two shadowy shapes. Yelled at Abby and the pilot, and we flew closer. It was a massive blue whale and a smaller one, cruising north. We flew by several times to watch them. It was brilliant! They made several shallow dives every 20 seconds (I counted 18 dives in all), then a deeper dive of half an hour. Feel so lucky – there are probably only around 6,000 to 14,000 left in the <u>whole</u> of the world's oceans...

MY BLUE WHALES!!!
Probably a mother and her calf returning north, to breeding grounds

Conserving the Antarctic

Since 1961, Antarctica has been protected by the Antarctic Treaty, which aims to safeguard the continent from exploitation, reserving it for peaceful scientific work. In 1991, a Protocol on Environmental Protection banned oil- and mineral-mining in Antarctica for 50 years. However, many countries are keen to exploit Antarctica's rich resources, or use its biological reserves, such as commercially harvesting krill for food. Such steps would seriously pollute the continent and damage its ecosystem. Organizations such as Greenpeace are working to have Antarctica declared a World Park, so that it can never be mined or exploited.

McMurdo station – a scientific research station, on Ross Island, Antarctica.

Whaling

Since it began around 1,000 years ago, whaling has taken the lives of millions of whales, and today there is probably no more than 5–10% of the original great whale population left on Earth. Whaling is now regulated by the International Whaling Commission (IWC). Although there is a ban on the commercial killing of whales, some countries, particularly Norway and Japan, still hunt them. Several species of whales are recovering; others, such as the northern right whale, may yet become extinct.

Local Alaskan whalers tow in a bowhead whale. The IWC allows them to catch about 60 whales a year.

Things to do back home

- Help save the whales! (Join a conservation group and write a letter of protest about continued whaling)
- Find out where I can practice snorkeling!
- Look up these whale web sites. ↗
- Find out what I need to do to become an oceanographer! (check the Internet)

Whale web sites

http://www.friendsoftheocean.org/ (to sponsor whales, dolphins, or sea turtles)

http://www.oceanalliance.org/index.html (organization dedicated to the conservation of whales)

http://whales.magna.com.au/home.html (plenty of information on whales, with lots of pictures)

GLOSSARY

abyssal plain Wide and fairly flat area of ocean floor, which has an average sea depth of about 13,000 ft. (4,000 m). These plains develop between volcanically active regions where sediment – made up of sand, mud, volcanic dust, bits of shell, and tiny skeletons – builds up and covers the hills and valleys of the ocean floor.

algae (singular: alga) Simple plants made up of one, several, or many cells with no true stems, roots, or leaves. Most algae grow in fresh water and the sea, although some live in damp soil and on tree trunks.

Antarctic The cold region south of the Antarctic Circle. It includes the continent of Antarctica and part of the Southern Ocean.

Arctic The cold region north of the Arctic Circle. It includes the North Polar pack ice, most of the Arctic Ocean, and the most northern parts of Eurasia and North America.

baleen Bony comblike fringe hanging down from the upper jaws of a baleen or toothless whale. The baleen strains small crustaceans from seawater taken in the whale's mouth. The whale has to shut its mouth to squeeze the water through the baleen.

bathyscaphe The earliest diving vessel that could withstand the great water pressures of the deep sea.

bivalve An animal, such as a clam, razorshell, mussel, or other mollusk, with a soft body and a pair of hinged shells that can be opened and closed.

bony fish Fish with a bony skeleton, such as a cod or tuna. Bony fish are the most numerous fish in the sea.

brittlestar Relative of the starfish with long, thin arms; belongs to the group of invertebrates called echinoderms.

cartilaginous fish Fish with a skeleton made entirely of cartilage, a gristly, elastic substance.

continental rise Mound of sediment settling on the sea floor at the base of the continental slope.

continental shelf The edge, or rim, of an ocean basin that drops away from the shallows of the seaside to a depth of about 650 ft. (200 m).

continental slope Steep slope descending from the continental shelf to the abyssal plain on the ocean floor.

copepod Tiny shrimplike crustacean; important member of the zooplankton.

coral Hard substance formed as an external skeleton by tiny marine creatures called polyps. When the polyps die, their skeletons build up to form coral reefs.

crust Rocky "skin" that forms a thin shell over the Earth's surface, forming the continents (continental crust) and the ocean floor (oceanic crust).

crustacean Invertebrate with jointed legs and a tough chalky outer skeleton (called an exoskeleton); includes such animals as crabs, lobsters, and shrimp.

decapod 10-legged crustacean. Most decapods have 10 main limbs (four pairs for walking or swimming, and one pair of pincers to pick up food). Decapods include lobsters, crawfish, crabs, and shrimp.

demersal Referring to animals, particularly fish, that live on or near the bottom of the sea.

echinoderm Member of an invertebrate group that includes sea urchins, starfish, brittlestars, feather stars, and sea cucumbers. All share three characteristics – a body arranged in parts of five, a skeleton of plates embedded in the skin, and tube feet operated by hydraulic pressure. The name comes from the Greek *echino* meaning spiny and *derm* meaning skin.

filter-feeder Creature such as a mussel or limpet that strains food from water.

food chain A chain, or sequence, of living things linked by the things they eat and the things that eat them.

food web Several overlapping and connected food chains.

invertebrate Animal without a vertebral column (backbone). Invertebrates include sponges, cnidarians (such as jellyfish, sea anemones, and corals), mollusks (such as limpets, clams, and squid), echinoderms (such as starfish, sea urchins, and sea cucumbers) and crustaceans (such as barnacles, shrimp, lobsters, and crabs).

jellyfish Cnidarian with stinging tentacles that drifts on ocean currents.

larvae (singular: larva) Name given to the young of an animal, such as a crab, that looks very different from the adult form.

mammal An animal that breathes air, has hair, is warm-blooded, has a backbone, and feeds its young on milk. Whales and dolphins are mammals even though they are mainly hairless, with just a few bristly hairs on their heads.

mantle Rocky middle layer of the Earth, between the crust and the core, or center.

migration Journey made by an animal to breeding grounds or to find food. Many journeys are yearly, but some happen only once in an animal's lifetime.

metamorphosis A complete change of physical form. Metamorphosis is more common in invertebrates than vertebrate animals.

mollusk Invertebrate with a soft body, and a chalky shell in one or two parts. Mollusks include bivalves, such as cockles, scallops, clams, and mussels; gastropods, such as sea slugs; and cephalopods, such as squid and octopus.

oceanographer Scientist who studies the ocean and marine wildlife. Oceanography is the science of studying the oceans.

ooze Name given to the type of sediment on the ocean floor that is made up of the remains of animals and plant plankton. Ooze may be hundreds or even thousands of feet thick.

photosynthesis The process by which plants, trees, and some bacteria trap sunlight energy and convert it to make their own food.

plankton Microscopic plants (phytoplankton) and animals (zooplankton) that float in seawater.

polyp Animal with a trunk-shaped, soft body topped by a mouth surrounded by a ring of tentacles.

predator Animal that hunts and kills other animals for food.

prey Animal that is hunted and killed by other animals for food.

remotely operated vehicle (ROV) An unmanned robotic diving vehicle that is operated by remote control from a submersible or ship.

sea Another name used for "ocean," or a named part of an ocean. For example, the Mediterranean Sea, the Sargasso Sea, and the Caribbean Sea are either part of, or connected to, the Atlantic Ocean.

sea cucumber Cucumberlike marine invertebrate; a type of echinoderm.

sponge Simple animal with a hollow body and no head, limbs, or gut. Most sponges live on the seabed.

squid Mollusk with ten arms, related to the octopus. Swims by forcing water out of its body through a narrow tube, propelling itself backward through the water.

submersible A small, manned underwater vehicle that is used for deepsea research and observation.

symbiosis When two dissimilar organisms live closely together in a symbiotic relationship, to the advantage of one or both, and harmful to neither.

tentacle Long, flexible structure, often around an animal's mouth, used for touching or for seizing food.

tide Regular rise and fall of the waters in the oceans due to the pull of the Moon and Sun's gravity.

upwelling A rising to the sea surface of cold seawater, which is full of nutrients, from deep in the ocean.

water pressure Weight of water over a given area. The deeper the water, the higher the water pressure. On the sea surface, the pressure is around 14.7 pounds per square inch (10,000 newtons per square meter), or one atmosphere. Water pressure increases with depth at one atmosphere every 30 ft. (10 m). At the deepest part of the ocean (at the bottom of the Mariana Trench), the water pressure is more than 1,100 atmospheres. Some sea creatures have adapted to withstand this incredible pressure. Humans would be squashed to a pulp.

wobbegong, tessellated A carpet shark that has a patterned (this is why it is called "tessellated") brown and white skin.

THINGS TO DO

• VISIT AN AQUARIUM OR AN OCEAN PARK

Look up local aquariums or an ocean center near you. Some may have special open days when you can get up close to sharks, dolphins, or other sea creatures.

• GO COASTAL WILDLIFE WATCHING

Winter or summer, visiting the coast can be an great adventure! Take along an identification guide, inspect small tidal rockpools for fish and crabs, and watch for seals on the rocks. Always tell an adult where you are going and what time you are going to return. Better still, go with an adult or a friend.

• STUDY A ROCKPOOL

Next time you go to the beach, take along a snorkel mask so you can dip your head into the water in a rockpool and study sea creatures without hurting them. Be as quiet and still as possible, and you may spot a fish or crab hiding in cracks between the rocks. The best time for looking in rockpools is when the tide is going out or has just gone out – but always keep watch to make sure you don't get cut off by the incoming tide.
It's also a good idea to wear trainers or hiking shoes so you don't cut your feet on sharp rocks or shells.

• VISIT AN ESTUARY

Estuaries are places where fresh river water meets salty seawater. Take your time and be patient, and you should be rewarded by seeing lots of birds, fish, and mammals.

• LEARN HOW TO SNORKEL

You'll need a mask, a snorkel, and fins – and somewhere safe to practice. Get an instruction book to show you how, but only try if you're already a pretty good swimmer.

• JOIN A CONSERVATION GROUP

Write to one of the organizations listed on this page or visit their web site.

• MAKE A SEASHELL COLLECTION

Collect shells next time you're at the beach, but make sure there is no conservation order first (check first to find out. If there is a conservation order for a particular beach or area, you cannot take any of the shells) and take them only if they're not occupied. Keep your shells in a clear glass jar or vase filled with water, or glue them on a piece of wood or in the top of a shoe box to display them. If you want to make them shine, rub a little mineral (not cooking) oil into the shells, (but don't varnish them). Label the shells with the place you found them, the date, and the name. (Check in a guide to try to identify each shell – you could add a "?" after any name you are unsure about.)

USEFUL ADDRESSES

American Museum of
Natural History
Central Park West 79th Street
New York,
NY 10024
www.amnh.org

National Museum of
Natural History
Smithsonian Institution
Washington, DC
www.mnh.si.edu

Scripps Institution of Oceanography
University of California
San Diego
California
www.sio.ucsd.edu

Natural History Musuem
of Los Angeles
Los Angeles
California

Friends of the Earth (USA)
The Global Building
1025 Vermont Avenue, NW
Suite 300
Washington, DC 20005

Greenpeace Inc (USA)
1436 U Street, NW
Washington, DC 20009
www.greenpeaceusa.org

National Geographic Society
17th and M Streets, NW
Washington, DC 20036
www.nationalgeographic.com
(publishes National Geographic Magazine (adults) and National Geographic World (ages 8+)

National Willife Federation
1400 16th Street, NW
Washington, DC 20036-2266
(publishes Ranger Rick (ages 6–12)

The Cousteau Society, Inc
870 Greenbrief Cricle
Suite 402
Chesapeake, VA 23320
Tel: (800) 441-4395
www.cousteausociety.org
(publishes Dolphin Log (ages 7–15)

WEB SITES

http://oceanlink.island.net/
Plenty of information on oceanography, marine mammals, seabirds, fish, and marine pollution. With an "ask a marine scientist" section.

http://www.wdcs.org/wdcs/index.htm
Whale and Dolphin Conservation Society homepage; supports research into and conservation of cetaceans.

http://www.northcoastmarinemammal.org/
Find out how this center in northern California helps injured seals, whales, and other marine mammals; has a kids, fun section.

http://www.divediscover.whoi.edu/
Read all about deepsea exploration with scientists cruising the mid-ocean ridge. Find out about underwater volcanoes, black smokers, and strange sea creatures.

http://www.wh.whoi.edu/faq/index.html
For loads of information on fish – fish facts, lots of fish questions and answers, from "do fish sleep" to "how do you estimate out the age of a fish. Put on the net by Northeast Fisheries Science Center.

INDEX

ACKNOWLEDGEMENTS

PICTURE CREDITS

Photography by Dave King

Photomontages by Ella Butler

Maps by Alan Collinson Design

Other art by: Graham Allen; Bob Bampton (Bernard Thornton Artists); Robin Boutell (Wildlife Art); Keith Brewer; Jim Channell (Bernard Thornton Artists); Malcolm Ellis (Bernard Thornton Artists); Mike Foster (Maltings Partnership); Peter Hayman; Gary Hincks; Steve Kirk; Alan Male (Linden Artists); Colin Newman (Bernard Thornton Artists); Obin; Peter Sarson; Dick Twinney; Michael Woods

PHOTOGRAPHIC CREDITS

l=left; r=right; b=bottom; t=top; c=center
All photography by Dave King except:
6-7 David Lomax/Robert Harding Picture Library; 8 A.N.T./NHPA; 9 ESA TSADO/Tom Stack & Associates/NHPA; 10-11 (photomontage) Heather Angel, Dan Burton/BBC Natural History Unit,Jason Smalley/BBC Natural History Unit, Leo Batten/Frank Lane Picture Agency, N.A. Callow/NHPA, Laurie Campbell/NHPA, Daniel Heuclin/NHPA, David Boyle/Animals Animals/Oxford Scientific Films & Paul Kay/Oxford Scientific Films; 12t Paul Kay/Oxford Scientific Films, 12b Douglas Peebles /Corbis; 13t Bill Coster/NHPA, 13c Eric Woods/Oxford Scientific Films, 13b Ben Osborne/Oxford Scientific Films; 14 Harold Taylor ABIPP/Oxford Scientific Films; 16-17 (Photomontage) P. Morris/Ardea, Ron & Valerie Taylor/Ardea, David Hall/BBC Natural History Unit, Brandon D. Cole/Corbis, Digital Vision, Henry Ausloos/NHPA, A.P. Barnes/NHPA, Bill Coster/NHPA, Mark Deeble & Victoria Stone/Oxford Scientific Films, Paul Kay/Oxford Scientific Films & Kim Westerskov/Oxford Scientific Films; 18tl David A. Northcott /Corbis, 18tr Tom Brakefield/Corbis, 18b Tom Walmsley/BBC Natural History Unit; 20t Rodger Jackman/Oxford Scientific Films, 20b Howard Hall/Oxford Scientific Films; 23 N.R. Coulton/NHPA; 24-25 (Photomontage) Heather Angel, Peter Herring/Natural Visions, Nature Focus/Australian Museum, Norbert Wu/NHPA, Peter Parks/Oxford Scientific Films & Norbert Wu/Oxford Scientific Films; 27 Norbert Wu/NHPA; 28-29 (Photomontage) B. Jones & M. Shimlock/NHPA, Kevin Schafer/NHPA, Norbert Wu/NHPA, David Fleethham/Oxford Scientific Films, Rudie Kuiter/Oxford Scientific Films, Peter Parks/Oxford Scientific Films, Gerard Soury/Oxford Scientific Films & A. Witte & C. Mahaney/Tony Stone; 33t S Summerhays/Biofotos, 33b Trevor McDonald/NHPA; 34-35 (Photomontage) Anthony Bannister/NHPA, Sarah Cunliffe/Oxford Scientific Films, Ken Smith Laboratory Scripps Institute of Oceanography/Oxford Scientific Films & Woods Hole Oceanographic Institution; 36 Ralph White/Corbis; 38-39 (Photomontage) Jean-Paul Ferrero/Ardea, Doug Allan/BBC Natural History Unit, Perry Conway/Corbis, B & C Alexander/NHPA, Rod Planck/NHPA, Dr. Eckart Pott/NHPA, Doug Allan/Oxford Scientific Films, Rick Price/Oxford Scientific Films & Steve Turner/Oxford Scientic Films; 40 Daniel J. Cox/Oxford Scientific Films; 42 Stan Minasian/Frank Lane Picture Agency; 43 Galen Rowell/Corbis
Cover photography by Dave King except for the following: Pilot whale: David A. Northcott /Corbis; Bottlenose dolphins: Tom Brakefield/Corbis

A Marshall Edition
Edited and designed by
Marshall Editions Ltd
The Orangery
161 New Bond Street
London W1S 2UF
www.marshallpublishing.com

Original concept by Sue Nicholson

Published by Tangerine Press™, an imprint of Scholastic Inc.
555 Broadway
New York, New York 10012

Tangerine Press™ and associated logos and design are trademarks of Scholastic Inc.

Originated in Italy by Articolor
Printed and bound in Italy by Officine Grafiche de Agostini
10 9 8 7 6 5 4 3 2 1

ISBN 0-439-31688-X

Consultant:	Trevor Day
Editors:	Claire Sipi and Scarlett O'Hara
Designers:	Penny Lamprell and Siân Williams
Jacket Designer:	Steve Woosnam-Savage
Editorial Manager:	Kate Phelps
Art Director:	Simon Webb
Publishing Director:	Linda Cole
Proofreader:	Jane Chapman
Indexer:	Jean Clarke
Production:	Christina Schuster
Picture Researcher:	Su Alexander
Research:	Julia March